Rē•Bound

A Collection of Family Reflections

<u>Authors</u>
Dr. William B. Martin II
William Blain Martin III
LaQuenta V. Martin
Christina Martin

P3 Life, Inc.
Los Angeles County | California
www.themartinfamilylegacy.com

Copyright © 2023 by P3 Life, Inc.

All rights reserved. This book is protected by the copyright laws of the United States of America. This book may not be copied or printed for commercial gain or profit. The use of short quotations or occasional page copying for personal or group study is permitted and encouraged. Permission may be granted upon request.

Dedications

This book is dedicated to every family unit that wants to overcome the past and reunify their family unit.

"I honor the wife of my life, Delores Florene Holland Martin who has stood by my side through thick and thin. She has always offered her support, cheering us on to finish the task of writing this book. You are truly loved and appreciated."
- Dr. William B. Martin II

"I am inspired daily by my family. My Queen Brittiny, my two young Kings William Blain IV and John Cameron and my little Princess Ny'a Brielle. If we have another addition to the family, he or she will be a part of my daily inspiration. Every decision I make, every action I take is always to benefit and enhance our family name. My writings are dedicated to you guys. You are my motivation in life."
- William Blain Martin III

"To God. You renew me abundantly.
I am nothing without you.
My beginning. My boldness. My capacity. My cup filler. Nothing energizes me like your divine essence and power.
Everything works for my good in your powerful plan.
Every connection flows from you, every gift is for you.
In your majestic tender love, I am whole, fearless and free.

I stand today, walking in your natural greatness, giving you all honor and glory.
To my parents, I am forever thankful that you created a foundational home of leadership and learning. Thank you for raising me to be a woman that understands the Spirit of Our Creator, the depth of faith and core cost of love.

To my Big Bro and Baby Sis, you know my tears and my triumphs. Thank you for being my rocks of honesty, as a sibling trio. Our bond has become unbreakably tight from PKs to adulting we have supported each other in transparent growth and tough transitions. Our roots run deep, our love runs deeper.
p.s. Thanks for making me "Auntie Q".

To those I love, my extended family, circle of cousins, soRHOrs and the best "foodie" friends in the world - thanks for getting me out of the house to dance or throw axes, sending funny reels/memes, sharing stories over tacos, joining me at the gym, pushing my military style workouts, and the quality time of fun travel & companionship. You are the sacred village around me, sending words of affirmation, laughter on stressful days, celebrating and supporting my journey of pursuits & endeavors. I treasure you all.

This book is for my sonshines,
Lyriq Jalon & Aidan Langston and the angel baby I carried but never got a chance to hold - you have given me purpose.
I promise to always speak and write in truth to you.

*Being your Mommy is the most extraordinary gift from above, in motherhood I build my legacy.
I am intentional and unstoppable to prepare and make a path for you...You remain my reasons to rē•bound in life.
- LaQuenta V. Martin*

*"I dedicate this to my future family. I hope this becomes a tool full of resources, inspiration and encouragement to each member at a time of need."
- Christina Martin*

*<u>Special dedication from the Martin siblings:</u>
This book was written with special dedication to the heart and soul of the Martin Family, the late Dr. Deborah Verness Hardy-Martin. We love and miss you every day, Mama. We still feel your presence. We know you are very proud of us, bragging about us to all the angels in heaven. Thank you for instilling the principle of Love and Unity to guide our decisions and how we care for one another as a family. We will continue to honor your legacy, Mama.*

Acknowledgments

I must acknowledge family members who have made an indelible impression upon my life.

First and foremost are my beloved parents, William Blain Martin, Sr. and Ruth Lee Gosey Martin whose legacy continues to be celebrated throughout the pages of this book.

Secondly, my brother, the one and only Sherry Ford Martin, who has always shown his support for me and our family. His example has influenced the lives of our entire family. He is a living legend with an amazing testimony of faith, demonstrating excellence and integrity in life. His skillful entrepreneurship has produced a successful business that has gained the attention of youth worldwide. Nothing has altered his commitment to be the best that he can be with absolutely no excuse for failure.

Thirdly, I pay tribute to my only sister and brother in love, Billy James Turner and Ruth Marie Turner. They were always supportive and offered whatever they could to show their love in word and deed. They will never be forgotten and their legacy lives on through their descendants.
- Dr. William B. Martin II

Sincere gratitude to Dr. C. for editing, formatting and writing the foreword for this book.
- From Martin Family

Foreword

As you peruse this precious and timely book, you will glean from the nuggets of wisdom that have been expertly inserted within the ten chapters. The members of the Martin family "dared" to be transparent about their individual and collective life journeys in an effort to assist families in their times of family and personal ordeals, including heartache, trouble, despair, quests, goal setting, and even during their triumphant moments. The Martins' writings demonstrate a strong desire and need for love and unity, which they each had the courage and tenacity to seek after and for which to strive.

Each chapter illuminates a personal journey that caused the particular author to ask hard questions while being engaged in a determined search for answers. The transparent conveyance of the journey is breathtaking, refreshing, and reassuring.

The bravery displayed within these pages will usher you into a condition of bravery as well, giving you a desire to face your trials, challenges, and incongruences head on. Your bravery coupled with God's Word that is interweaved throughout the narratives will give you the lift you need to persevere.

As I read, one specific truth became abundantly clear: The transparency and words of wisdom contained within will bless readers for generations to come.

In admiration,
Dr. C.

Table of Contents

Introduction   **11**

Chapter One   **13**
     Rē•bound

Chapter Two   **21**
     Rē•born

Chapter Three   **29**
     Rē•lationship

Chapter Four   **43**
     Rē•store

Chapter Five   **49**
     Rē•flection

Chapter Six   **55**
     Rē•duce

Chapter Seven   **69**
     Rē•direct

Chapter Eight   **77**
     Rē•evaluate

Chapter Nine 87
> *Rē•structure*

Chapter Ten 99
> *Rē•building*

Introduction

"For whatever things were written before were for our learning."
(Romans 15:4, NJKV)

As the head of the Martin family, my purpose for writing is to educate, encourage and empower you the reader that rebounding in life occurs when you realize that this too will pass. Therefore, regardless of whatever happens in life, you can overcome anything, anytime, and anywhere by God's grace.

- Dr. William B. Martin II

"He has made everything beautiful in its time."
(Ecclesiastes 3:11, NKJV)

Our family collectively came together and decided to begin our writings for this book during the COVID-19 pandemic. It was our opportunity to share with others that they can discover how to **rē•bound** when all hell breaks out in their life. In these unprecedented times, a word of faith and family support will ensure victory when faced with uncertain times, situations or circumstances happening in this world.

This book was written to journal our thoughts on how we rebounded as a family after going through disappointments, dilemmas, and distant relationships. We needed to figure out how to **rē•store** trust through open dialogue and **rē•build** belief. For our family, it started six years ago when we had a conference call on a Saturday morning to discuss the health of our mother. To this date, we continue to have our family conference calls every Saturday morning. During one of our calls amidst the pandemic, we decided we should write a book together and share our thoughts on family ordeals in an effort to help other families.

In this book, you will read the perspectives of each family member on "rē" words that have helped in finding love and unity. You will read our personal intimate thoughts about ourselves and each other with biblical and real-life references (***denoted by an asterisk****). It is our hope that your family will be able to use the principles we learned from life experiences that divided us, then by God's grace **rē•connected** and **rē•strengthened** us through honesty and forgiveness. Please read our family collection of life's reflections.

- The Martin siblings (Will, LaQuenta, & Christina)

Let's begin... Shall we?

CHAPTER ONE

Rē•bound

Dr. William B. Martin II

> **Rē•bound** (verb) – the ability to recover or reclaim after a sudden setback or disappointment.

Rebounding from Life's Setbacks

The word **rē•bound** has many definitions. You are probably thinking of a basketball play or stat but the word actually has more meaning. Webster's dictionary states, "to rē•cover in value, amount, or strength after a previous decrease or decline." It also has reference to taking back possession of something lost, but the definition that really empowers the word states, "to rē•cover from some sort of setback that causes frustration."

The question is, "Can you bounce back from a setback?"

Are you in a position to come back after a setback has occurred?

You may be thinking, *What do I do next?*

Have you ever been in a position to come back after a setback has occurred?

Accept What Has Happened

When setbacks occur, accept what's happened in your life. Then, put what has happened behind you. Let it all go. Have faith that good things are coming your way.

Give Yourself Time to Heal

Everything heals. Your body heals. Your heart heals. The mind heals. Wounds heal. Your happiness is always going to come back. Hard times don't last.

Forgive Yourself and Others

Setbacks can injure you and cause hurt for a while. Forgiving those who have hurt you and forgiving yourself is the key to regaining victory. Maya Angelou said, "It's one of the greatest gifts you can give yourself, to forgive. Forgive everybody."

Learn From Your Experience

It has been said, "The beauty of life is that while we can't undo what is done, we can see it, understand it, learn from it, and change it." You can learn great things from your mistakes when you aren't busy denying them.

Formulate a Plan

Creating an action plan begins with having a clear vision. When setbacks take place, your plan will move you in the direction of accomplishing your goal. With a well-designed plan, you can achieve virtually anything you set out to do.

Expect to Come Back From a Setback

God can turn any setback into your greatest comeback yet. Everyone loves a good comeback story. But without a setback, those comebacks wouldn't be possible. You are in the driver's seat. Take control of your emotions. Develop a belief system by walking and talking about the results. It should be noted that to **rē•bound** naturally, one must first **rē•bound** spiritually.

Spiritual rebounds are comebacks from circumstances and situations that come into all of our lives. These occurrences can bring about flashbacks. Once a setback takes place, there will be people, even family members, who will try to hold us back, remind us of that instance or even throw back the obstacle in our pathway. We have to be prepared to put back into practice the things needed to overcome the mistakes we all make. We can switch back instead of sitting back and letting things get worse. Giving back is a secret weapon during times of loss where we share our testimony to encourage and strengthen those in need.

Rē•bounds are comebacks from flashbacks that throw-back.

Rē•bounds are the take backs in life that provide another opportunity for success.

Setbacks

Setbacks happen to each of us in life. These encounters in life can be major or minor. A setback by definition is an interruption in progress. It is a problem that delays or prevents progress or makes things worse than they were, as a speed bump in the middle of the road. Setbacks make things harder to accomplish but should never be viewed as the end of the road. A dead end simply means turning around and going in the opposite direction to reach your destination.

Setbacks are opportunities for comebacks.

Setbacks can hold up your destiny.

Setbacks provide feedback for your future direction in life.

We hope these collections of writings will show families how we came together to face challenges and disappointments rather than doing so separately. As you continue to read through this short book of principles, you and your family will be able to better handle whatever curveballs life throws your way. No matter what's going on, no matter what has happened, and no matter what struggles or setbacks you are currently facing in life, our prayer is that we can reach your heart, as you read or listen to these chapters.

We intend to provide new insight and perspective on how to cope and maneuver when life seems to deal a bad hand or unexpected circumstance. To you, we present our journey using several **"rē"** words to implement into your life. With use of these words, as a family, we were able "to rē•store trust and rē•build belief," or as we like to call it **"Rē•bound."**

In this book, you will find **Reflect** pages with lines at the end of each chapter. This is where you can journal to explore your own **rē•bound** journey. Studies show that one of the best ways to deal with any change, challenge, or emotion is to find a healthy way to express yourself like writing. Our family has found this to be true.

We hope this book becomes a tool of transparency...
- to track your triggers
- to face your fears
- to manage your mental health

We invite you to enjoy the experience.

May you capture your thoughts, gain closeness with those you love, gain strength to cope in difficult seasons, and ultimately create a space to rē•set your mind. May you find peace over problems as you plan, prepare and progress in the world and have hope for a higher vision of positivity to **rē•bound** in your life.

Reflect

The Martin Family

CHAPTER TWO

Rē•born

Dr. William B. Martin II

> **Rē•born** (verb) – to be brought back to life or activity

Rē•born has reference to having experienced a complete spiritual change. Similar words for **rē•born** include reboot, rebound, recovered, reformed, remanded, and renewed. If you say someone or something has been **rē•born**, you mean he/she has become active again after a period of being inactive. Since no one has the chance to experience his/her physical birth a second time, to be **rē•born** means to undergo a meaningful spiritual change.

Every human being goes through the process of being **rē•born**. The born-again experience is a part of every aspect of life. Being born anew or born from above is the essence of rebirth. In certain Christian churches, congregants choose a time to be baptized or ritually admitted to the church, and it's at that moment they consider themselves to be **rē•born**. This idea is rooted in the New Testament where Jesus says, *"No one can see the kingdom of God unless they are born again"* (John 3:5).

The point is this, being born is not something you have anything to do with. You didn't have anything to do with your physical birth, nor do you have anything to do with your spiritual birth. Being born physically is something that happened to you that is completely out of your control. So, being spiritually born is something that happened to you that is also completely out of your control.

In both cases, God created you by the means of your parents, but God created you. Your parents could give you physicality, but only God could create your spirit. And in the spiritual sense, being born again is an act of God by which He recreates you. It's a new birth. And that's the point of the simple analogy.

*At the age of five years old, I played the role of a minister in a Tom Thumb wedding. I officiated over the wedding where two children, my same age, played the role of bride and groom. This was an event in my life I will never forget.

- *Why was I selected to act out this role?*
- *What did this mean?"*
- *How would this make an impact on my life?*

I pondered over these questions and received answers throughout my life. Playing the role of a minister at that age was not a coincidence. As I look back over my life, that became a defining moment. I was told by those who put on the event that I had the qualities of a minister. They shared that I exhibited signs that caused them to select me for the role. Looking back, I can honestly say I felt comfortable in that role.

It didn't seem as though I was acting. In reality, that was the beginning of my life's calling. At eight years old, I had a life-changing experience. I received a series of visions of Christ at various times. I remember a particular vision of the suffering Christ on the cross. It was horrific.

His body was beaten beyond human recognition. It was hard to witness, and I cried because of what I saw. The vision led me to decide to accept Jesus Christ as my personal Lord and Savior. At the age of eight, I was baptized and came up out of the water praising God for the wonderful experience. I began to recognize God was dealing with me. Something was happening that was out of my control. It was my new birth: a born-again experience that changed my life right before my eyes.*

Here is an inspired poem I wrote:

Divine Restart

It was a restart
Like a finished work of art
That began deep in my heart
And I promise never to depart
I am called to play this part
Thank God I made a smart decision
Hallelujah, it's a brand new start.
Things were not the same,
So now I am focused and taking aim
Because I realize that this change in life is no game
Satan has come and is trying to blame and shame

But I will continue and maintain my frame
And give God the glory, praising His Holy name.

A divine restart is going back and beginning all over. It's starting again, spirit, soul, and body. It's like pushing the "Reset Button." Some wall outlets have a small red button in the middle. It's placed there in case the power goes out. It is to be used in case the electrical current shuts down. The little red Reset Button is to restore power to the outlet at a time when needed. That's an illustration of what happens in our lives. Sometimes, things just shut down. Situations and circum-stances can sap our energy and enthusiasm for life.

It is with the heart that man believes unto righteousness or right standing with God according to Romans 10:10b. Usually it's not a head problem but a heart problem we are dealing with. There comes a time for us to surrender, give up our ways, and let God have His way. The power we need to overcome in this life is supplied by our Power Source, the Holy Spirit. He is our Reset Button.

We should remember that in life, we gain control or we lose control. Being in control is the position most people like to be in. Conversely, losing control is not a position any of us are accustomed to being in.

Here is an illustration that may shed some light. A computer's keyboard has different functions available to the user. The keys allow for options to be activated by their particular function. There are three keys that when used at the same time will alter the computer's function. They are CONTROL, ALT, and DELETE.

The CONTROL button when pressed with another key performs a special operation.

The ALT button when touched allows access to another level, shifting into another dimension.

The DELETE button when activated eliminates the actions previously taken.

When these three keys are pressed simultaneously, the action allows a shortcut keyboard function that will end an application's task. This action will cause the computer to shut down and restart what you were previously working on.

Everyone, from the womb to the tomb, can thank God for our new birth. The caterpillar spins a silk cocoon from its mouth while preparing for its change of life. It then surrounds itself with the silk, making a cocoon to close out the world around it. Then over time, an inward change occurs, and a beautiful moth comes to life and flies away. So, the caterpillar that used to crawl around on the ground in its previous life miraculously changes and is introduced to a brand new world. So, you don't come out the same way you went into it. When we experience a rebirth, we are not the same. Then, we can see what to do, act on that knowledge, and experience life in a brand-new way.

In John 10:10, the Greek word for life is Zoe. It means the Abundant Life. It's life with an advantage. That's the new life that comes from rebirth.

Here's another inspired poem I wrote:

God Has More for Us

God has more for us
God loves us that's for sure
And He begins within our inner core
Telling us to get up off the floor
And when it looks like it's over, He opens up the door
So we can walk through it, receiving benefits galore
That's why we must always ignore
Satan tries to convince us, that we deserve to be poor
A divine outpour is what God has in store
For those who dare to swim, and leave the shore
So don't worry about the score
Go on the sleep, it's ok to snore
When you wake up, you will realize,
God has made us for so much more.

In summary, rebirth is more than a conversion; it's a new beginning: the attainment of a new life from the old man into a new man. Remade means to be made again or anew. It is to be renovated, revised, made over, or redone. **Rē•born** has a reference to being brought back to life or activity. It's having experienced a complete spiritual change. Receive your rebirth, a process of remaking and being reborn all over again, inwardly and outwardly.

Reflect

The Martin Family

CHAPTER THREE
Rē•lationship

Dr. William B. Martin II

> **Rē•lationship** (verb) – a family in the following manner: A family is a group of two people or more related by birth, marriage or adoption and residing together

Family Relationship

A family is a specific group consisting of people who may be made up of partners, children, parents, aunts, uncles, cousins, and grandparents. It is made up of all the descendants who share common ancestors. The term "family" is from the Latin word "familia," which includes (encompasses) the parents and children living together in a household.

The traditional family is a family structure that consists of a man, a woman, and one or more of their biological or adopted children. Family is important because it provides love, support, and a framework of values to each of its members. Family members teach each other, serve one another, and share life's joys and sorrows. From their first moments of life, children depend on parents and family to protect them and provide for their needs.

A family is a group of people who love each other. There may well be moments when not everyone likes each other, but love will always be there. A real family shows kindness and respect to one another. They may argue and disagree, but remembering that love is present means they will figure it out. The best thing about family is we know we have each other's back. We remember we all are living this life to face everything together. The support, love, and affection you get from your family are the best things, and you can't ask for more.

The biblical definition of the family is the foundational institution of society ordained by God. It is the fundamental institution of human society.

*We were the picture-perfect family. The first family of the church. Our motto was family first, focus on the family. We intended to present publicly how a Christian family looks. We were a minister's family, whose kids were PKs (preacher's kids). But what happened disturbed our connection as a family unit. Unfortunately, our family was torn apart by divorce after twenty-five years of marriage. That interrupted our family unity. It took its toll on all of us. Our lives were greatly affected.

Christina was the youngest and took it very hard. LaQuenta had just graduated from high school and internalized the situation. Will began to isolate himself and tried to handle it alone. We were all hurting and didn't know which way to turn.

Communication was difficult because there was nothing to talk about. Things had been done. Decisions had been made. Feelings were sporadic, and emotions were running high.

Advice was given to me in the form of an illustration: If a mud ball is thrown at you, try to dodge it, so it won't hit you. But if that mud ball lands on your clothes, don't wipe it off immediately, for it will smear all over you. Give it time to dry. Then, once it has dried, brush it off. There will be a mud mark, but it won't leave a permanent stain.

Our family **rē•lationship** had been disturbed. I arranged for professional counseling. It greatly helped and laid a foundation for healing and restoration. We still were far from being able to interact with one another. Lines had been drawn and sides taken, which caused conflict and confusion. But time eventually brought about a change in attitudes and actions. Each of us needed a revival within. It took years for our family to be brought back together. God enabled us to make it by taking it one day at a time.

Our entire family was experiencing hard times (good times and sad times), but we made it by the grace of God. It was a divine rebound. A comeback from a setback. We bounced back after being thrown up against the walls of adversity. God gave us the strength to go on. It was difficult, and there were times it seemed as though we weren't going to recover. But, we did because of the Lord who was on our side. He promised never to leave us alone.

I wrote praise songs as a means of comfort and stability during those times:

"He promised, promised me

Never to leave me alone."
Hebrews 13:5

"Be strong in the Lord
And in the power of His might
For we wrestle not against
the flesh and blood of man
But against principalities
We have the weapons to defeat the evil one
We can stand
And take command."
Ephesians 6:10-12

Kingdom Man of God Wanted

God is calling for a man who will stand in the gap. A Man who will give himself to prayer and the ministry of the Word of God on behalf of his family. Standing in the gap relates to a man interceding for his family, community, city, state, and nation for the will of God to be done.

1. *A man who will follow the map.* The Word of God is our map and will provide us with a lamp unto our feet and a light unto our pathway. David said thy word have I hid in my heart that I might not sin against thee (Psalm 119:11, NKJV). Jesus said, *"Man shall not live by bread alone but by every word that comes from the mouth of God"* (Matthew 4:4, NKJV).

2. *Man must learn how to rap.* This means living by the Word speaking, thinking, and believing what God's Word says

becomes vital for victorious living as a man of God. Just because one may be of the male species does not make him a man. In today's society, there is mass confusion as to the masculinity of men. Recent legislation has determined from a secular standpoint that manhood is a matter of civil rights. There is a definite difference between a Kingdom Man of God and the rest of mankind. The prophet Ezekiel cried out for a Kingdom Man of God, so He would not have to destroy a people. Today, we are lacking Kingdom Men of God and, as a result, we are destroying ourselves.

Statistics on fatherlessness in America:
- Roughly 70% of all prisoners come from fatherless homes
- 80% of all rapists come from fatherless homes
- Fatherless homes produce 71% of high school dropouts and 63% of teen suicides.

A Kingdom Man of God is every man's destiny and every woman's dream! When a Kingdom Man of God steps out of his door each day, heaven, earth, and hell take notice. A Kingdom Man of God zeros in on one purpose and one purpose only: advancing the Kingdom for the betterment of those within it, which glorifies the King!

God has a standard. He has a goal. His Kingdom is that goal. Yet, many men have lowered their standards. The results of a low standard affect us all. It starts locally, then spreads regionally, grows nationally, and destroys culture around the world. Just look around at our homes, churches, communities, and world to discover that men - maybe most men- have missed the goal to live as Kingdom Men of God. Husbands and fathers need to know how to comply with the biblical standard God is calling men to within the home. The standard by which women should long for, children need, and men are constantly trying to achieve is God's standard.

> *"Then God said, 'Let Us make Man in our image, according to Our likeness, and let them rule over the fish of the sea and the birds of the sky and the cattle and all the earth, and over every creeping thing that creeps on the earth.'"*
> (Genesis 1:26, NKJV)

Adam was the original man created by God to have dominion over His creation. The Lord put His first man Adam in the garden of Eden to dress it and keep it. Man was told not to eat of the tree of knowledge of good and evil, for if he ate, he would surely die. Adam committed high treason against God.

> *"For as by one man's disobedience many were made sinners, so by the obedience of one shall many be made righteous."*
> (Romans 5:19, NKJV)

> *"And the Lord God called and said, 'Adam, where are you?'"*
> (Genesis 3:9, NKJV)

Adam lost control of his domain shortly after having received it. He was silent when he should have spoken up as the man. God was calling for a leader, but Adam stood by while the serpent conversed with his wife and when he allowed that to happen, dominion was lost over God's creation.

Fathers, where are you? Fathers must recognize God's purpose for their family is to reflect His kingdom (Genesis 1:28-30).
1. Fathers must believe God wants to display His triune image through their families (Genesis 1:27-28).
2. Fathers must submit to the rule of God because he is the head of the family (Exodus 34:23-24).
3. Fathers must understand Satan's schemes, so they can protect their family from his attack (Genesis 3:8-14).

Remember, as Kingdom Men of God, you should declare: As for me and my house, we will serve the Lord!

A tribute poem to fathers:
Father's Day started in 1909 with a young lady whose name was
Sorona Smart Dodd
She was inspired to honor her father with more than a simple
gesture or common nod
Her father, Henry Jackson Smart was a single parent who raised
her according to the Word of God
Brother Smart was a Civil War veteran and farmer known for the
goodness of his heart,
Liken unto a potter molding his clay into a vessel, a work of art
Likewise, a true father is a man with a plan,
who will not fall into sinking sand
Living life according to God's command,

claiming victory, and possessing the land
I recall my father, a good man who worked hard
and did the best that he could
A true inspiration and example of the meaning of Fatherhood.
- Dedicated to my dad, William B. Martin Sr.

*I take being a Kingdom Man very seriously. My life is dedicated to representing Christ in our society today. As a father, I have endeavored to exhibit the following characteristics before my family:

1. Integrity
2. Courage
3. Legacy
4. Wisdom
5. Love
6. Fruit
7. Truth

A song I wrote some time ago says:

We are Men that Win, Men that Win
Men with dominion over sin
With Christ as our Lord
We'll make it to the end
We are Men that Win
We are winners and with Christ we have victory.
We are winners and Jesus is Lord.
"A father of the fatherless, a defender of widows."
(Psalm 68:5, NKJV)

> *"As a father pities his children, so the Lord pities those who fear Him."*
> (Psalm 103:13, NKJV)

Here are some qualities a father should also possess:
1. All good parenting begins with the fear of the Lord.
2. Fathers set the tone for their household. Make sure your God is at the center of your family.
3. Teach your children to lead their lives based on a biblical worldview.
4. Remember, your choices and actions will impact your children and their children's children.
5. Talk to your children about the Bible and help them to learn scripture. Use scripture as the basis for your parenting.
6. God cares about the **rē•lationship** between fathers and their children.

*My **rē•lationship** with my children has greatly improved. We have a weekly conference call to communicate what is going on in our lives. Our effort to make sure this weekly dialogue is continued takes personal diligence on our part. Looking forward to hearing the praise reports, testimonies, and updates provides an atmosphere of unity and support enabling us to face another week with confidence.

This didn't happen overnight. It took a concerted effort to educate, encourage, empower, and evaluate the overall sacrifice that it would take to commit to such an endeavor. My heart's desire has been fulfilled by seeing our family share openly with one another in love, seeking to provide assistance with whatever we all are going through. This is a family **rē•lationship** by example. We are determined to share this experience with everyone. There is no excuse for failure in this vital area.

Dr. Martin Luther King said, *"The ultimate measure of a man is not where he stands in moments of comfort and convenience, but where he stands at times of challenge and controversy."*

There are many "ships" of life we have all taken during our time here on earth.

Rē•lationship
How two individuals regard and behave toward each other.

Companionship
The enjoyment of spending time with someone or other people.

Fellowship
The friendly association of a group of people meeting to pursue a shared interest.

Friendship
The **rē•lationship** of mutual affection between people who like each other and enjoy one another's company.

Discipleship

One who embraces and assists in spreading the teaching of another.

Leadership
The ability of an individual to lead or guide in a particular area.

Kinship
The way in which people are related by birth, marriage, or adoption.

Mentorship
The guidance provided by an especially experienced person.

Stewardship
The careful management of something entrusted to one's care.

Citizenship
The status of a person recognized under the custom or law as being a legal member of a nation.

Hardship
A situation when your life suffers adversity from something difficult or unpleasant that you must endure or overcome.

Workmanship
The work and skill that goes into making something.

Worship

The expression of reverence and adoration for God.

Ownership
The state or fact of exclusive rights and control over personal property, any asset, land, or real estate.

Rulership
A position in which one rules over something.

Salesmanship
The skills and methods used in selling or promoting products.

> "We may have all come on different ships,
> but we're in the same boat now."
> Dr. Martin Luther King, Jr.

> "Whatever your life's work is, do it well.
> A man should do his job so well that the living,
> the dead, and the unborn could do it no better."
> Dr. Martin Luther King, Jr.

Reflect

Rē•Bound: A Collection of Family Reflections

The Martin Family

CHAPTER FOUR
Rē•store

Dr. William B. Martin II

> **Rē•store** (verb) - to give back (someone or something that was lost or taken); to return (someone or something); to put or bring (something) back into existence or use; to return (something) to an earlier or original condition by repairing it, cleaning it

The following simple sentences are used to illustrate the usage of the term "**rē•store**."

1. He desires to end your misfortunes and **rē•store** you to your home and family.

2. He hurried to find the family of that civil servant to **rē•store** the daughter to her mother and go to save someone else.

Restoration is the act of repairing or renewing something. An example of restoration is remodeling an old house to its original state. Another perspective showing what restoration is likened to is giving someone his/her job back.

> "Incline your ear, and come to me. Hear, and your soul shall live; And I will make an everlasting covenant with you - The sure mercies of David. Indeed I have given him as a witness to the people. A leader and commander for the people. Surely you shall call a nation you do not know, And nations who do not know you shall run to you, Because of the Lord your God, And the Holy One of Israel; For He has glorified you. Seek Lord while He may be found, Call upon Him while He is near.
> Let the wicked forsake his way, And the unrighteous man his thoughts; Let him RETURN to the LORD, And He will have mercy on him; And to our God, For He will abundantly pardon. So shall My word be that goes forth from My mouth; It shall not RETURN to Me void, But it shall accomplish what I please, And it shall prosper in the thing for which I sent it."
> (Isaiah 55:3-7, 11; NKJV)

> "Have mercy upon me, O God, According to Your lovingkindness; According to the multitude of your tender mercies, Blot out my transgressions. WASH me thoroughly from my iniquity. And CLEANSE me from my sin. PURGE me with hyssop, and I shall be clean; WASH me, and I shall be whiter than snow. MAKE me hear joy and gladness, That the bones You have broken may rejoice. CREATE in me a clean heart, O God, And RENEW a steadfast spirit within me. RESTORE to me the joy of your salvation, And uphold me by your generous Spirit. DELIVER me from the guilt of

bloodshed, O God, The God of my salvation, And my tongue shall sing aloud of your righteousness."
(Psalm 51:2, 7-8, 10, 12, 14; NKJV)

Steps to Comebacks

1. Don't Dwell on Mistakes

The term "dwell" means to think or talk about something for a long time.

Mistakes are learning experiences that allow you to evolve as a person.

Mistakes can be turned into miracles over time.

Stop thinking about what has happened to you.

Overthinking is not healthy. Look at the mistake you made as a stepping stone to bettering yourself for the future. Make the decision to move on to other endeavors.

Everyone makes mistakes in life, but that doesn't mean he/she has to pay for them for the rest of his/her life. Sometimes, good people make bad choices. It doesn't mean they're bad people. It means they're human.

Remember these things:

You can't have a better tomorrow if you're always thinking about yesterday.

Don't dwell on mistakes, because they will only cause more.

Don't carry your mistakes around with you. Instead, place them under your feet and use them as stepping stones. Never regret. If it's good, it's wonderful. If it's bad, it's experience.

Zig Ziglar said, *"Don't let mistakes and disappointments of the past control and direct your future."*

2. Get Off the Deck

There are times we all need a check-up from the neck up. Our attitude determines our altitude. Negative thinking can truly hinder our ability to move on in life. To rē•bound, we must get off the ground. No more frowns from feeling down. What happened was meant to keep you bound, so decide to get off that merry-go-round. It's time to get down to business and expect to abound. Those times of being lost have turned around. So, look around and expect to be crowned because you have been set up for your rē•bound.

3. What's in Your Wallet?

The nation's largest direct bank has been promoting its credit card services by asking this question. It is an advertising slogan that has gained popularity since the year 2000. Now, twenty years later, it is the 13th most well-known slogan of all time.

That brings me to share the value of your personal slogan for your life. How does your slogan help you? A slogan is a group of words that clearly advertises a brand or company's mission, its core values, and what it has to offer. A slogan sums up what your life is all about in a short, catchy way. It shows your creativity, and above all, communicates your value to the world. Our life slogan is essential in leading a successful life. We live in a world of competition, and that edge of having a personal slogan can be all it takes to make a difference. After facing a life encounter, speaking your way back to life and health is vitally important. A key benefit of a positive slogan is boasting about how you can improve the lives of others rather than being stuck on self-promotion. Words that release positive emotions have a longer-lasting effect than those that release negative emotions.

Reflect

_____

_____

_____

_____

_____

_____

_____

The Martin Family

CHAPTER FIVE
Rē•flection

Dr. William B. Martin II

> **Rē•flection** (verb) - to give evidence of the character or quality of something

*Over the course of my life, I have had many setbacks. Despite whatever has come, I have overcome by the grace of God. As I reflect over the years, I still wonder how I made it.

If you look in a mirror, you will see your reflected image.

Reflecting also means seeing something original in another form or image. The Word of God is like a mirror.

"For if you listen to the word and don't obey, it is like glancing at your face in a mirror. You see yourself, walk away, and forget what you look like. But if you look carefully into the perfect law that sets you free, and if you do what it says and don't forget what you heard, then God will bless you for doing it."
(James 1:23-25, NLT)

Anytime you look into a mirror, you see yourself. The mirror doesn't lie but reveals the way things are. Our lives are better because of the application of the Word of God. Being a doer of the Word literally means to become a performer of the Word. Being a hearer of the Word means being a pretender. In other words, one who is like a masquerader, impersonator, or imposter. People who are fakers put on a bluff, such as counterfeiters, charlatans, and hypocrites.

"Just to hear the Jewish law does not make a man right with God. The man right with God is the one who obeys."
(Romans 2:13, NLSB)

"The time will come when people will not listen to the truth. They will look for teachers who will tell them only what they want to hear. They will not listen to the truth. Instead, they will listen to stories made up by men."
(2 Timothy 4:3, NLSB)

Many world champion athletes, business people, and spiritual leaders all cite self-reflection as an essential key to their success. This is also true for everyday people who are fulfilled and happy with their lives.

Self-reflection is defined as meditation or serious thought about one's character, actions, and motives. It's about taking a step back and reflecting on your life, behavior, and beliefs. Remember, insanity is doing the same thing over and over again but expecting different results. **Rē•flection** allows you to respond not react and provides a clear perspective.

In our past, we see our failures, our enemies, our victories, and our defeats. The past allows people of the present and the future to learn without having to endure. We can see how others coped. We can see that others survived hard times. The past gives us the courage to go on to a bright future.

Here are some outstanding quotes to remember:

*"Life can only be understood backward,
but it must be lived forwards."*
Soren Kierkegaard

"Reflect upon your present blessings of which every man has many, not on your past misfortunes, of which all men have some."
Charles Dickens

"Without deep reflection, one knows from daily life that one exists for other people."
Albert Einstein

"Our language is a reflection of ourselves."
Cesar Chavez

*"Whenever you find yourself on the side of the majority,
it is time to pause and reflect."*
Mark Twain

*"If we are to go forward, we must go back and rediscover
those precious values - that all reality hinges on a moral
foundation, and that all reality has spiritual control."*
Dr. Martin Luther King, Jr.

"There is no greater harm than that of time wasted."
Michelangelo

*"Logic will get you from A to Z;
imagination will get you everywhere."*
Albert Einstein

Reflect

The Martin Family

CHAPTER SIX
Rē•duce

LaQuenta V. Martin

> **Rē•duce** (verb) - to cause a gradual decrease, make smaller or less in amount, diminish in degree, size, or importance

I quit!
I don't wanna do it!
I need a break!

That's how I would feel on the days I was overwhelmed. And, it was during those moments when I knew I needed to identify the reason I was stressed. That's when I would do a mental brainstorm. That's when I'd write things down, get restructured, and **rē•duce** what was going on in my head.

Have you ever had moments when you asked yourself, "What am I going to tackle first?"

Have you ever had a headache, felt fatigued and sleepy, or had tears streaming down your face, but you could not figure out exactly why?

Have you ever been moody or had a bad temper with the people you love?

When does your patience wear out?

Do you know these feelings? Yeah, these emotions are indicators. They're signals. That's when it's time to take a pause and **rē•duce** what's going on in your mind and your heart.

I would always know it was time to **rē•duce** the mental stress in my life when I was unclear about what to do next when making a big decision, or it became really difficult - even confusing - to **rē•duce** all my options and choices, so I could be on a clear path. This is what I have noticed in the process of dealing with mental overload. The choices aren't simple. Often, we need help to gain clarity.

When I was in a relationship with a narcissist, he had an addiction that he kept hidden. I didn't know what to do even though I didn't like the situation. I tried discussions over dinner, prayer, and even leaving. After talking to him about finances and noticing the pattern of lies about where he was, I became detached. While dealing with the stress of motherhood while raising our sons, maintaining my class grades in a graduate degree program, and realizing the extreme incompatibility, I experienced hair loss and weight gain from both sadness and stress at the same time. We had a miscarriage. That angel baby was lost and so was the love between us. The next few years became a blur. We didn't speak much; we only collaborated to be a blended family. As a stepmom, I wanted our sons to be raised together.

I craved salty foods and sweets. I chose to eat them often. I became heavily involved in church and community organizations just to be busy. I wasn't treating my body or mind with kindness or self-care. The beautiful thing is a mentor stepped into my life, and we discussed things I hadn't under-stood about love and compassion. I learned about authenticity and emotional intelligence. I realized through counseling that I had to work on myself and become a better woman. There were difficult days and arguments; it got ugly. That was when I needed my support system to rē•bound. I opened up to my family, and they helped me get past the difficult days.

And, let me be honest. Stress and feeling overwhelmed are not easy topics to discuss, especially if people are accustomed to being upbeat and positive. Mental strain or depression can be taboo and unfamiliar topics for friends and family to understand. However, the more we connect closely in a vulnerable moment, they can detect when we are under pressure if a strong bond exists.

But, in many families, we can ignore each other or become caught up in life without checking on each other. We forget to ask if everything is okay. Other times, when loved ones reach out, we wear a mask. We're not open about what's going on in our lives. Or worse, when we are asked, "How are you doing?" we tell a lie. We keep it hidden in dark places because we may not think they'll understand, or we feel we shouldn't burden others with our thoughts, issues, or problems.

But, we actually can all benefit from being vulnerable. It connects relationships together and eases the mind. Most of all, true self-care is having a consistent space to unload, regain clear thoughts, and receive feedback. The best decision any of us can make is to have a check-up session with ourselves in a healthy format, such as therapy, life coaching, or counseling with a professional to assist us, so we can sort out our thoughts in a series of sessions. These conversations can open doors to help us navigate the mind and identify what is the root of stress or mental strain.

Time Wasted

Some of us are busy bodies. I know I am. When I set a goal, I put energy into completing it. When I don't have an area to focus on, I feel stagnant. However, in other times, I've met people who stay in motion all the time, yet they are indecisive. This can impact what they finish; they have all the ideas but struggle with planning and execution. Procrastinators are a whole different breed of humanity. They rather put off what they don't enjoy or choose to avoid doing a little at a time, then take action on everything at once. That causes time to be compressed (and compounded with frustration). That is ultimately when we overload ourselves. Perhaps, it is from running a business, raising children, taking care of personal projects, managing multiple clients, or taking on a demanding work or school schedule. Ask yourself, "What takes the majority of my time?"

In my life, there have been seasons when I placed too many things on my to-do list. Then, I found myself frustrated when I only crossed one thing off. How about you?

Some people can slowly and strategically put together a plan, and they only concentrate on one thing at a time. However, many others find that time floats by as they move from one idea to the next. That's the real struggle; that's the one I have faced. I multitask, and I overload. I make lists, so I can map out time. I make a schedule, so I do not waste valuable hours. However, there are moments I still feel mad at myself when I need to complete a project, but I have already allowed myself to take on too much too fast. By then, I cannot give my best. My mind decides it doesn't want to keep up the pace, process, or compute another solution.

Have you ever been stuck, completely overwhelmed, or find it difficult to tackle another creative task? I've learned over these past years that there's no peace in that process. I've learned that when I take my time, slow down, and reduce what I am doing or what I am focusing on, I can produce better quality and even accomplish much more. Time is valuable; we have to designate, define, and protect our time.

Tangible Things

So, this word **rē•duce** means a lot to me. For many reasons, I've had to learn, unlearn, and relearn what it means to **rē•duce** my focus and even **rē•duce** what I own. Sometimes, our possessions will make us feel very heavy and bound. We need to **rē•duce** what we have and manage everything, from finances to furniture. The more you have, the more there is to take care of. That's why we need a mindset to **rē•bound** and refresh, renew our minds, and **rē•duce** what we do from day to day and hour to hour.

Now, you may be wondering - *How do I begin to reduce what I'm doing and all the items I own? How much do I take on?*

This has been an ongoing life lesson I've noticed in people I encounter, those I coach, and the people I welcome close into my life. Even acquaintances I have observed from a distance have helped me to see how we all need to **rē•duce** our responsibilities. It's an epidemic. We spend our energy over-loading our plates, and some teach our children to do the same.

We measure our importance by promotions, positions, vacations, graduations, and business achievements. We post our accomplishments on social media for recognition and burn ourselves out and waste time looking for validation in our success by how much we do. But, honestly, we all could benefit from a more simplified life.

One summer, I knew I needed to **rē•duce** everything. I had accumulated a lot of clothes. I thought to myself, *Q, this will come back in style.* But, either my style changes or my weight does, so I end up keeping items that should be given away. Over the past six years, since my divorce, I've carried things from one place to another. When I chose to move out of state, I needed to load my U-Haul to travel from Nevada back to California. I had a two-bedroom apartment, and I had collected enough household items to fill a five-bedroom two-story home.

I procrastinated (completely wasted time), left myself less than a week to pack, and gave away as much as I could, but there were still multiple bookshelves, desks, lamps, and too many shoes and clothes in the closet. Boxes stacked to the ceiling and bags of food and vitamins from my pantry (many that were expired) created a hot mess for me to stress over. My loving family helped me clear things out. I had my dad, brother, two nephews, uncle, and best friend all helping me plus three professional movers. I was overwhelmed the entire time.

Here's my "list of failures" from the situation:
1. I failed to plan (to schedule, create a timeline, and set priorities).
2. I failed to ask for help sooner (to get extra hands for a big project).
3. I failed to downsize (to make the move easier).

Why do people struggle to **rē•duce** the number of items they have in their possession?

I buy more than I need because I never want to run out of what I have. When it comes to soap, shampoo, or laundry detergent, I buy two or three at a time. During the COVID-19 pandemic, it really got crazy. When I didn't think I could get to a store, I started buying in bulk (and not even with coupons). I was paying full price. I ordered cases of hand sanitizer, toilet paper, paper towels, paper plates, plastic spoons, and forks. I seriously loaded up all my cabinets, and I bought a freezer chest to store meat. I stocked up on deodorant and toothpaste.

But, it didn't end there. I became a shopaholic online, ordering multiple colors of the same sweater or leggings, and it was terrible trying to make it all fit in my apartment. I was mad at myself when I saw my credit card balance rise, and I was mad at my space because I felt it was limiting me from buying more. I have met many other people who constantly shop, and I watch tv shows about hoarders. But that time, I was the one with the problem, and I began to address the reasons.

To me, buying too much means you're concerned about lack and have a fear of scarcity. It can expose a controlling area of your personality or mean you haven't had much control in the past. Perhaps, you have lived with someone who exerted dominance or aggression. Maybe, in childhood you lost a sense of appreciation for something. For instance, I had a collection of electronics: multiple tablets, cell phones, and laptops that were outdated or no longer in use. If my son broke one or it showed signs of malfunction, I would replace the item, but I would not get rid of the broken device. During my move, sorting through things to give away to Goodwill or to sell online became frustrating.

When I saw everything I had, the phrase "out of sight out of mind" became my reality. Items were hidden in cabinets, drawers, and containers. I was mad because I had so many different sets of ankle weights, barbells, and even a broken trampoline. I looked around my home, and there was so much to get rid of that my mind became full and overwhelmed. I became physically tired from thinking about what to do with all the crap.

What Happens When We Don't Rē•duce?

So, that brings me to point number two. When we don't **rē•duce** what we have, what we are thinking about, and what we need to do in one day or one hour, our body responds. Mental overload creates fatigue. Sometimes, it leads to headaches or cramps. Other times, we might just cry, take a shot, pour a glass of wine, or light up a cigarette. But those are not the best ways to process; they are unhealthy. So, what should we do? Relax. Meditate and listen to music, go for a walk outdoors, connect with nature, or take a nap. Find a life coach or therapist to work through the matrix of your mind. **Rē•duce** what you focus on.

*Back to my story. On the moving weekend, I was in a space of extreme mental exhaustion. Sick of seeing boxes and thinking, "LaQuenta, you're a clutter magnet." I had accumulated items very quickly. The overhaul process was not easy to face because I had hoarded a lot of stuff. But, it was time to **rē•duce** in a big way. That's exactly what I did. My family helped me get rid of all the junk. We filled an entire dumpster, so I could only travel with necessities. It was a lighter way to roll to my next destination. It felt good. It took me trusting my family, so they could help me through it with care and compassion.

Putting it all together:
How will I know when it's time to **rē•duce** what I manage?

Your body will demand that you slow down. Your mind will start to ache from thinking. Some people get sick - high blood pressure, ulcers, chronic migraines. There are so many indicators depending on the stressful nature of your home, work, relationship and how you choose to unplug.

In my career, I've worked in management and education for over seventeen years in many roles from the credentialed teacher, to the program coordinator, to the student services advisor, to the college professor, to vice principal. Often in my positions, I have to figure out solutions on the spot - for classroom instruction, absent teacher coverage, student disruptions or campus safety, addressing the compassion fatigue teachers deal with trying to inspire learners to care and remain engaged. Every day is a battle; there's a different issue or problem to solve. When my mother became increasingly ill and then she transitioned, I could no longer handle the weight or pressure of work and the grief from loss happening in my heart. My body was telling me my gas tank was empty, and I needed some time off to refuel.

Some days are hard; others are even more challenging and complex. Each day is a new set of issues. It's difficult to address any of this when your body is not in the best condition. Let's face it, we all deal with issues. In my world of education, it may be to help learners become future graduates or parents dealing with unemployment or grief at home, address complaints about the school, or assist students who break down crying because of what they personally deal with in life.

I realized very early in my career that people were hurting and wanted to talk about it: the students, the teachers, the parents, all of them. And it's overwhelming at times. I can't solve everything. But, I can **rē•duce** how much I take on at a time. That's why this word means so much to me.

Some days can bring scattered thoughts, lack of motivation, or simply wanting to stay in bed. I remember many days when I wanted to be moving faster. But, I was too tired. I was fatigued and wanted to just stand still or be still from all the running around - chasing what? I was fatigued from doing everything, all the time managing my children, my business, and my own life, too. I was tired from all the energy I spent taking care of those around me. Yet, I knew I needed to focus on what I could control and work to plan, pursue, and execute my responsibilities and goals.

I was running webinars, creating eBooks, recording podcasts, planning my next business moves, cooking/meal planning, shopping for groceries, or doing endless laundry. Everything felt heavy. I felt as though I had grown past the point of carrying all that it took to maintain where I currently stood, and it was daunting.

When we expand beyond the point of the pot in which we are planted, we need to transplant. With so many new ideas and talents and the next steps, it's easy to be frazzled or frustrated. That's when I required assistance. I received great advice to rebound out of the feeling that I had to take care of it all. I started pre-cooking meals for days at a time and took my clothes to a fluff-and-fold service to get assistance with laundry. I learned it's better to be resourceful and have peace. Let's practice the art of choosing to **rē•duce...** or get ready, because what you store away and pile up can eventually tumble on you.

Our Mind, Our Time, Our Things

Do you have a process for coping with all of the thoughts in your mind?

Do you set boundaries and control your energy flow, so time isn't wasted?

Do you know which things in your life need to stay and which need to go away?

It may be time to **rē•duce** into a minimalist lifestyle.

Ask yourself:
- Why do I struggle to give items away?
- What do I need to **rē•duce** in my life?
- Who can help me with the process?

In the past, I've had to consider what I'm feeling and decide if it was worth holding onto. We don't want to be emotional hoarders that do not know when to let go. So, we have to ask ourselves:

- Do I have too much stuff?
- Are there habits or patterns tied to emotions?
- Do I waste time when I am dealing with emotional triggers?

Depending on how you answered these questions, it may be time to **rē•duce** any mental or tangible limitations that may be in opposition to your forward progress and redirect your focus. Otherwise, the obstacles will not allow you to rebound to your next goal.

> "Manifest plainness, embrace simplicity, reduce selfishness and have few desires."
> L. Tzu

Reflect

The Martin Family

CHAPTER SEVEN

Rē•direct

Christina Martin

> **Rē•direct** (verb) - to direct again; change direction or focus

Imagine taking a car ride to a destination. You have entered your location into the GPS. You are on the road, and everything looks good. Traffic is moving. Then, your navigation system abruptly says, "**Rē•directing**." What? Why?

*I can only speak for myself, but a flood of emotions occurs when I hear this alarming voice. I'm flustered, unsettled, and worried to name a few. All I'm thinking about is I just want to get to my destination as quickly as possible with little to no problems. It seemed as though the trip was going to be a breeze. I planned things out in advance, I checked the traffic, and I even looked up the weather before I got on the road. Yet, here I am being told to change my course.

Ask yourself:
- *What do I do in uncontrollable situations?*
- *How do I typically respond?*

*This takes me back to when I learned to drive as a teenager. I was taught to be an informed driver. Meaning, before I get on the road, I should have an idea of where I'm going. Researching this will tell me the best time and route to travel.

I remember when my mother enrolled me in driving school to prepare me for my behind-the-wheel test. In driving school, I learned various driving hand signals and took copious notes to ensure I would pass my test. All of the information did not sink in, so my dad, who ironically was a driving instructor, gave me one-on-one lessons. He told me the fastest way to a destination is a straight line, and he taught me how to be a "defensive" driver. I enjoyed how my dad was calm when I would drive. He boosted my confidence as a young driver and was the best example of a co-pilot.

I had another family member who offered to teach me how to drive and that experience was much different. He would help me sharpen my driving skills with different road challenges. For example, he would have me take back roads, not use maps for guidance, and drive in various weather conditions. I hated it because it was stressful and just nerve-wracking. Knowing what I know now, the family member wanted to teach me to be adaptable to change. I didn't understand it then; however, I still carry those same principles in life today.

Ask yourself:
- *How has my family played a positive role in my life journey?*
- *Do I have an experience that has deepened my bond with the family?*

I did some research on how a Global Positioning System (GPS) works while giving guidance on the road. The GPS navigation process is more complicated than I thought. There are three main technology parts: satellites, ground stations, and receivers. On a map, three main indicators help you identify your placement and position point on earth: longitude, latitude, and altitude. Sometimes in life, we need to use our own "GPS" to stop and identify where we are in life before we can "map out" where we want to go. This is the starting point of gaining direction.

Let me explain what I learned from my point of view. The GPS broadcasts signals, which reach a network of control stations used to monitor and collect information. The system then provides a few different routes for you to select from. Routes may differ based on the number of miles and the time of arrival, and it may even give you options to avoid certain aspects of the trip, such as toll roads or freeways. This makes driving to new places easy. But life is not like this. And some may think, *If only life could be this simple.* This is where family can help.

Our family members watch us grow and develop into who we are. We share a collection of memories. Like the GPS, a family can provide three things in life: security, stability, and support. As we learn to build trust, the family needs these essential elements:

safety, consistency, and reliability. Family can advise you to help you arrive at your target destination.

Ask yourself:
- *Does this description of GPS sound familiar to any relationships in my life?*

*That reminded me of my relationship with God. Okay, let's look at this from a different perspective. The "car drive" is your life, and the "GPS" are outside sources like family, friends, or even God. When we are on this ride of life, we often gather general knowledge of where we want to go, how long or far it is, and what time we desire to get there. It's rare we just get in the car and drive. Typically, we plan, we get instructions, and we do what it takes to have a successful trip. These are all things we can control to ensure we arrive at our destination; however, in life there are detours. Roads may be closed, or there may be an incident that causes delays. Sometimes, when these situations arise, we can become so headstrong that we reject all help and even sound advice that's offered. This happens for two reasons:
- We are embarrassed because we don't know something.
- We don't want to acknowledge we made a bad decision.

These responses take us back to the first question: "What do you do in uncontrollable situations?" Furthermore, why do you react the way you do? If we can realize the GPS is there to be of aid and not to just control, we could put our pride aside and find peace instead. Think of it as a lifeline!

Rē•direction from the wisdom of others is the quickest way to get to your destination.

Ask yourself:
- *Why do I use a GPS but question it?*
- *Am I sure how to get to the destination?*
- *Do I need confidence in my car ride of life?*

Here are some words of encouragement when you face moments when things are out of your control. That is the perfect time to submit and take a rest. This reminds me of the acronym F.R.O.G., which stands for: Fully Rely On God. When we learn lessons of wisdom, we now can look ahead for any harm or danger. The wisdom of God operates similarly. It provides a deep range of understanding from a higher altitude. It surveys the area, receives data, and shares information with you on where to go or how to get there.

It identifies pitfalls and potential delays and guides you on a path to allow you to keep moving. It will tell you to change your speed and alter your route to get you to your desired place. It can take you completely in a direction you never saw so you can get there sooner than expected. *"For I am the Lord your God who takes hold of your right hand and says to you, Do not fear; I will help you"* (Isaiah 41:13).

> *"Life is not a destination, it is a journey."*
> Unknown

"It's not about when you arrive but instead who you are when you arrive at your destination."
Christina Martin

Reflect

_____

_____

_____

_____

_____

_____

_____

_____

_____

Rē•Bound: A Collection of Family Reflections

The Martin Family

CHAPTER EIGHT
Rē•evaluate
William Blain Martin III

> **Rē•evaluate** (verb) - to form an idea of one's identity, value or meaning in life again.

So, what is your name?

Close your eyes. Think about walking into a room full of people whom you have never met. Someone approaches you and says: "Hi, how are you? My name is (fill in the blank). What's your name?" Do you answer with your first name, your middle name, your nickname, or with your last name with your title in front of it? Think about this for a moment. Why do we choose to give out a "certain" name depending on whom we are meeting? I'll tell you why. Because we want to *impress* others. We want to be *accepted* and *acknowledged* by this certain name. You see, no matter what you think, it all starts with a name.

I'm not quite sure if I heard this in a commercial, saw it in a magazine, or read a bumper sticker somewhere but since understanding my name is bigger than just me, I had to **rē•evaluate** my thoughts about myself for the sake of making introductions.

Let's start from the beginning. Your name is the first thing that was given to you by your birth parents. It carries weight, legacy, and solidification. I say this because without it, how would anyone know how to address you?

Now, think about this...

Many parents think about the name of their child even before they conceive the child. Some parents ponder during the pregnancy, and some don't decide until the child is born. There are so many backstories on how a person's name came to be.

Some have personal cultural or spiritual meanings; some are named after one of their parents, grandparents, or another family member. Some are named after a public or historical figure. Some names are given simply because the parent has a favorite "something" like a fancy car (Mercedes), a unique tree (Mahogany), a wonderful feeling (Joy), a special time or season of the year (Sunshine or Autumn), or even a concept or idea (Future or Harmony). Nonetheless, a name has value; it has a purpose; and, it is forever.

Let's go deeper. Ready?

Your name should be celebrated simply because of the day you were born and your particular name should be honored on the day you die and beyond, actually *"to infinity and beyond"* (one of my favorite lines from a classic Disney movie). All human beings regardless of race, cultural, or spiritual background will encounter the natural fate of death one day.

We all know our birthdate, right? I mean who doesn't look forward to celebrating the day they were born? It's a day to reflect, a day to re-group, re-set or even better yet **rē•evaluate** ourselves. At least in my opinion, a person should. Why wait until New Year's Eve or New Year's Day to do this? Why not write out your new goals on your birthday and celebrate your accomplishments from the year past? At the very least, make mental corrections for yourself to get better results, right?

In a perfect world, every goal is met, but because we are imperfect beings, they are not. Should you let that discourage you to the point that you give up? It shouldn't. It should encourage you to **rē•evaluate** and remeasure your goal and what better day than on your birthday! Think about how this simple yearly life assessment could work in your life and those around you.

- What if everyone on the planet did this until his/her last breath?
- How better off would we be mentally?
- How focused and driven would we all be?
- How much positive energy would be created in the world?

Think about it.

People would be clearer on their path, have more insight into what they need to do, and have more direction on where they want to go. It would be awesome right? I truly believe so. If we all spent more time focusing on the areas we control, how much power could we truly possess? How much further would we be along in life?

Think about it more.
- *Could your particular name make an impact on others?*
- *Could your name add value to others?*
- *Could your name be remembered for something?*

How many people do you personally know or have known that fit this description? Is it a public figure, a family member, a friend, a mentor, or is it you? Just as Dr. King said, *"Everybody can be great... because anybody can serve."* So, I ask you, who are you serving? Yes, it all starts with a name, but what message will your name convey when people hear it? That's the question we all must answer.

Wanna make your name great? Start serving.

This is what I believe matters most after we are born. It's finding out how I can serve others and how I can give back, not what I can get from others. This is what is missing in our daily lives and why it takes us so long to find out why we were born. The gift of serving gives us a sense of purpose. Those who serve are fulfilled. They are always full of life and energy. They see life from a different point of view.

Think about it. If we all serve others, would we have a need? What should we focus or re-focus our time on before it's too late?

Whomever is reading this chapter may not know that answer right now, but that's okay because I didn't either. However, the only question I could answer was, "How do I want my name to be remembered after my time is up?"

I submit to you that your destiny is established by how we serve others and not just ourselves. With that establishment, your name will be celebrated not just on your birthdate but more importantly on your death date. You will always be remembered, so why not spend your time working on your name being great by serving? This is one of my favorite quotes, and I intend to fulfill my purpose by simply living it out.

Legacy

*So, let's start with my name. My full name is William Blain Martin, III. Continuing the legacy of my late grandfather, William Blain Martin, Sr. whom we all called "Big Dad" growing up has become a prideful task. Hell, I must admit it didn't hit me until almost high school that my name was identical to my grandfather's because I never addressed him by his birth name. It was always "Big Dad," and I always called my dad, (William Blain Martin, II) simply "Hey, Dad." For the record, my boys call me "Dad," or they substitute it for the less common word "Father," but I'll get into those meanings later. Funny story here.

Now back to where I was. Okay, yes... My full name. Well, it wasn't until I started to see my grandfather and father sign their names on checks and letters that I started to take more pride in it. Other than George Foreman, how many other legacy names carry past the second generation? I'll wait... There could be more, but I surely didn't know any growing up, and it made me feel proud and a bit awkward at the same time.

I truly thank the Almighty God for blessing me with such a legacy name. I am a part of a lineage that is well respected and honored. I have my shortcomings that have disappointed my family, but the way I have learned and grown after facing those challenges has made my family proud of me. My family may have been unhappy with my actions, but they never made me feel unloved. It was during my lowest times in life that I had to learn to lean on my family and allow their love to enter, especially when I questioned God's love and the love I had for myself.

I don't know who will read these words, but I do know the power of love heals our pain. I can only hope if you are feeling hopeless and full of despair, you will soon find liberty through honest conversation and submitting to the fact you do not know it all nor control it all. That thinking is what ultimately led me to an extended vacation I didn't want to take - if you know what I mean. I am a product of my decisions and actions, and I can honestly say I fell into a depressed state of mind, played the victim role, and complained about everything. It would have been a never-ending cycle if I remained in that state of mind. It wasn't until I started to do and think differently that I started to see a change in my life. As I pushed through getting out my thoughts on paper with clarity, I reflected on my years of existence: forty-four to be exact by the time this book is released. I have come to realize there are only two most important days in anyone's life.

1. The day you were born
2. The day you realize why you were born.

It was during my time of incarceration that I truly realized why I was born. Reflecting has always brought clarity to my life. Writing is a way for me to cope with my thoughts and feelings when situations and circumstances occur.

Reflect

Rē•Bound: A Collection of Family Reflections

The Martin Family

CHAPTER NINE
Rē•structure
William Blain Martin III

> **Rē•structure** *(verb) - to organize differently; a plan to strengthen and restructure your life or organization*

Shall we begin now? Say this with me… "I'm restructuring my life."

*A bill collector. "Scam Likely" calls. (I know some of you have received this call more than once). They called every day at the same time. Usually, I would send the call to voicemail, but finally, I answered one call and told the person, "I'm sorry. I have nothing for you. I am restructuring my life RIGHT NOW!" And, I hung up.

Those words gave me the power to do something different. I was tired of the position I was in, the feeling I felt, and the impact of not being able to do or go where I wanted. It crippled me. At that moment, I said, "Enough is enough, William!" It's time to make a change (*Man in the Mirror* – Michael Jackson).

Start to **rē•structure** by asking yourself these three questions:
1. *What am I grateful for?*
2. *What have I learned about myself lately?*
3. *What do I want people to know about me?*

These answers will determine your legacy. These three things will determine if you're going to go to the next level. Over the years as I've grown, I have had to ask myself, "What am I doing with my time? How much effort am I putting in? How is my attitude?" These are not easy areas to be honest about, but when we begin to see where our energy goes, things start to make sense. Every day, I had to monitor myself.

Do I have a positive attitude, or do I have a negative attitude? Am I expecting good or bad things to happen? This is how we stay ready for opportunities. This is when life can start to respond to you. While I was incarcerated, I had plenty of time to think about what I was doing with my time. I had to take responsibility for how I spent my time and with whom. I had to accept the fact that if I didn't change my mindset and my environment, I would not be able to change my situation. It all starts with you. Your results are dictated by where you put your effort and energy. No matter what you want to accomplish, it will all be determined by three words. These three "E" words helped measure my success.

Here are the three words and corresponding questions that guided me to **rē•structure** my life.

1. **Effort:** *How much effort am I putting in?*

2. **Ethic:** *Is my work ethic measurable, or is it duplicatable?*
3. **Enthusiasm or Energy:** *Is my energy positive or negative? How am I approaching the situation?*

Seasons Change

The word **rē•structure** simply means to reorganize to operate more effectively. It means rebuilding from scratch. It's taking what you have and rethinking your plan, redrafting, and eliminating the processes that didn't work. This is how to come up with a new way to move forward. This is a part of life that we should do three to four times a year. Consider how seasons change: winter, spring, summer, and fall. Each season has its characteristics. In each season, many of us change our wardrobe or attire.

As we **rē•structure** our closets to match the season, we change our clothes to prepare for the upcoming weather. So, do a self-inventory of your life and determine what season you're in. Are you wearing the proper clothes? A woman would not wear a bikini in the winter or a fur coat in the summer. Think about it. What am I wearing? How am I showing to the world? What do people see when they see me? How do people feel when I'm around? The whole point is to make sure you consider the factors around you to determine the way you approach a situation. Make sure you "dress" for the occasion.

Importance of Family

The importance of family is critical because a family member, related or not, is someone who knows you inside and out. It's someone who can tell you about yourself in love. It's someone who can speak into your life with the intent to help you grow. A lot of times this can be dangerous because we can use this against one another. We play it as a card to manipulate and get things out of one another.

*I remember when I was young, I knew my mother's and my father's personalities. I remember I would ask my mother certain things that I wouldn't ask my dad because I knew I'd probably have a better chance of getting a "yes" from my mom. We all remember that right? Being a parent of three different individuals, two young men who are attending college, William and John, and one new addition to the family, my first girl, Ny'a Brielle, who hasn't even started preschool yet has challenged me to be the best version of myself daily.

I recall when "my boys" (yes, I still call them my boys even though they are both over eighteen years of age) were young and all the changes I went through learning how to parent them with their mother, while learning myself and learning how to be a husband. Even though the marriage was dissolved after five years, I was committed to being a present father in their lives. It was a struggle especially when they moved out of the state with their mother after our divorce.

The best part about parenting is waking up every day to watch your offspring grow into independent people. There are times I see myself in "my boys," and it puts a smile on my face. The moments made through growing pains are priceless. Watching a reflection of yourself inside another human being is quite a daily experience. I'm sure my father feels the same way about me and my sisters. From a young toddler, to an adolescent, to a teenager and young adult, what a journey!

I had to realize parenting is about adjusting. I had to learn to relate to my offspring differently because I found out the hard way that you can't parent each child the same. Parents have to evaluate what they need to do to help their children accomplish their goals. Parents must coach them, motivate or inspire them in different ways because of their personalities and how they are wired.

Unlike my siblings, I'm a bit biased because, after twenty years of being a parent to boys, I am now a parent to a little girl with my beautiful wife Brittiny. I'm excited because I've always wanted a little girl, but I also had no idea how it would be to raise her. I have cousins who have girls, and I see how they interact with their daughters. I have some friends who are girl dads, but I never could fully relate. I've even watched different YouTube video clips on child development at certain ages, not to mention I have read great books where I could find inspiration from other fathers who are parents of a girl.

One of my biggest inspirations comes from a person I'll never meet in person but wished I could have. The closest I will ever get is through his books, interview clips, and social media posts. He is my favorite NBA player, the late-great Kobe Bryant. Anyone who knows me understands I am a diehard Lakers fan; I bleed purple and gold. To see Kobe excel on and off the court is such an inspiration. His book *Mamba Mentality* really changed my perspective on how to approach life daily.

I've learned so many principles from Kobe just from watching and listening. Being drafted and remaining with one team for your whole career says a lot. It first shows you have to grow and mature as an individual. Learn how to lead by example by holding yourself accountable, then others. Next, become accustomed to the people on your team knowing them inside and out. What brings out their emotions, their energy, and their effort?

Like a basketball team, it should be the same approach with your family. You have to learn to collaborate, evaluate, and start to make the changes necessary to accomplish a goal as a family. A championship team is built off culture and identity, and so should a family. There should be goals, agendas, plans, and accountability to accomplish as an individual and collectively.

*In my own life, when I remarried and decided to move to Las Vegas and become a blended family, we had to learn to become one team. A newlywed couple nine years apart in age, my wife with no children and there I was with two young preteens twelve and fourteen years old at that time. We had many discussions, some together and some individually. We asked each other tough questions. We became honest with one another. It wasn't easy because we all had different thoughts and assumptions about how it would work. It took some inward searching and looking at past upbringing and behaviors that shaped our thoughts of how to be a family.

It took communication to bring us together. It took time to restore trust and rebuild belief due to past hurts, disappointments, and regrets. Only through proper communication, allowing the grace of God and the power of love to heal are we able to function as a unit. The hardest part about family is dealing with loss, not just physical loss but mental loss, financial loss, and emotional loss. Each carries its burden. We have found proper communication at the time of under-standing and open heart dialogue was the remedy to adjust and cope with the loss.

It's been quoted many times, "A family that prays together, stays together." My immediate family did not always have proper communication. There were times when we did not talk and check in with each other for weeks, sometimes months. Two years before our precious Mama, Dr. Deborah, transitioned to her heavenly home, our father came to my sisters and me, stressing the importance for the family to start communicating on a weekly basis, even though we all lived in different cities and states.

We established a weekly date and time for one hour to discuss our previous and upcoming weeks and talked about our challenges and struggles from work life to home life, prayer requests, individual goals and opportunities, and family emergencies. We have continued this weekly call even as this book is being written. It has been over six years now, and we will continue our weekly calls. Those calls helped us through tough times like divorce, life insurance coverage, business ideas, writing this book, co-parenting, child support and custody hearings, discussing mischievous teenagers, and the hardest for all of us, the process of caring for our mother while she battled different health challenges in her body. At one point, we even had to come up with a schedule where we all took turns spending time and caring for Mama.

From her dialysis treatment three times a week, weekly cancer treatments, discussing her Medi-Care issues, establishing power of attorney and will and testaments, doctor appointments, hiring in-home care nurses, assisted living arrangements, moving to a rest home and eventually hospice, where we as siblings were able to be with Mama at her bedside in smiles and tears taking one final photograph, knowing it was just a matter of time because our mother wanted to stop doing dialysis treatment, which the doctors always told us during the eleven years Mama was on dialysis that her faith kept her alive all that time.

Through it all, my sisters and I were there together with Mom while our dad supported us with weekly communication and prayer because he lived out of state. The most memorable moment during our mother's final physical week on earth was not just hearing our mother ask for some soul food after not eating for almost three days, but the photo we all took near her side where we are all smiling. (Thank you, Uncle Sherry, for being there and capturing that moment.) Our mother gave her last breath two days later. I truly believe God put it on my dad's heart for the family to come together weekly and start bonding through communication.

Laying our mother to rest, in Feb. 2019, was one of the hardest situations our family has had to deal with. Being together and talking about our feelings from losing Mama in her physical state has helped us process our grief. Those who attended our mother Dr. Deborah's Homegoing Memorial Service truly saw the effect she had on us and on many extended family and church members. We are still in awe and grateful for how much support and love we have received. This book is in dedication to Mama's life mantra, "Walk in Love & Unity."

As I close my thoughts on the word **rē-structure,** I truly believe my family saved my life. I have come to experience love in a greater fashion because of family. I have grown to be grateful and humble, never being too high or being too low.

I truly think about how I can be an impact to others I come across and what I can leave behind to help my family further progress in life. This is important to me because in life we will all go through things that will seem so overwhelming, so overbearing, and so complicated. No one should go through those moments alone; self-isolation or separation is not the way it was designed for a person to handle those situations.

God places families together in order to help each other out sincerely. We should embrace family, not disgrace family. But if we do, family should still be there with open arms to embrace in love and forgiveness. I needed it. I felt like I had disgraced my family and certainly disappointed them, but they never made me feel less than or abandoned. That's what I am most grateful for because I didn't deserve it. I truly thank God for my family because there was a time when I did not love myself, the person I had become, and I felt like I let the family down. They didn't tell me at my low point but built me up, so I could receive tough love. Then, they encouraged and challenged me to be better one day at a time and hold myself accountable for the small things first. It took all of these low experiences in my life for me to understand the power of love and unity and the importance of family.

You may not be ready to admit it or acknowledge it, but this is the only way to **rē-structure** your life. It starts with you. Results happen after constant consistency.

Questions to ask yourself:
- *What areas in my life need to be restructured?*
- *How do I manage my time and my money?*
- *Is it a job or a career choice or a business endeavor?*
- *Is it a personal or business relationship, a family member, or a co-worker?*
- *What do I control?*
- *What don't I control?*

Many people miss their opportunities because they're not ready because they haven't been practicing. They haven't thought about what they would do if an opportunity occurs. In the areas you do not have control over, you have to give it to someone outside of you. That could be another human being, or it could be a spiritual being. No matter the connection, who or what you believe, always reflect on what you can do better while thinking about where you are headed. That's my definition of **rē-structure**.

Reflect

The Martin Family

CHAPTER TEN
Rē•building
Dr. William B. Martin II

> **Rē•building** (verb) - a point, period, or step in a process. A part of an activity or a period of development.

An example of **rē•building** can refer to a project that is in its final stages and should be completed by August. Another illustrative statement is, "We are decorating the house in stages, so it won't be ready for another couple of months." I desire to approach this introduction in stages, dividing the activity of writing this book into parts and completing each chapter separately.

> *"I will restore the fortunes of my people Israel, and they shall rebuild the ruined cities and inhabit them; they shall plant vineyards and drink their wine, and they shall make gardens and eat their fruit."*
> (Amos 9:14, ESV)

"Then I related to them how the good hand of my God was on me and what the king had said to me. Then they replied, 'Let's begin rebuilding right away!' So they readied themselves for this good project."
(Nehemiah 2:18, NET)

"It will be a day for rebuilding your walls; on that day your boundary will be extended."
(Micah 7:11, NET)

The above verses of scripture reference the term **rē•building**. **Rē•building** is the process of building something again after it has been damaged or destroyed. It also can refer to the restoration of a system or situation to a previous condition.

There comes a time in all of our lives when we must take on the challenge of **rē•building**. This process of **rē•building** will come amid life's difficulties, which ultimately are designed to destroy your destiny.

The question is, *"What in your life needs **rē•building**?"*

Take time to reevaluate the extent of the renovation process of your life. What steps are you willing to take for the **rē•building** process to be completed? Where will your foundational support come from? How available and flexible are you in allowing the time it will take to finish the work in you? A commitment should be made to face yourself. Look in the mirror. Realize life is not over. Sure, there will be hills, valleys, mountains, and even rivers that must be crossed, but recognizing **rē•building** is a necessity. I can assure you it will be an uncomfortable journey, but with faith and patience, plan for the desired outcome.

One thing is for sure, you must forgive. This begins the healing process. It is a primary foundation so many fail to recognize; instead, they compromise to their destruction. Release and let go of past hurts and resentments.

Remember, anything you cannot control is out of your control. If you can't handle what is happening, then let God provide you with the wisdom and knowledge you need to go on. Let reconstruction continue with your eyes on the prize regardless of the size of the reconstruction project in your life. God can do amazing things with those who put their trust in Him. He knows what you can bear. So, don't be scared by the insurmountable task; just put on your mask and stand back for the blast of God's power to make things happen fast. Remove those who tear down your construction.

There will be haters and agitators who will come to watch and criticize your reconstruction. So, encourage yourself and rejoice during the process of **rē•building**, knowing it shall surely come to pass. Embrace with grace what you have to face. Remember, His grace is sufficient to see you through the trials and tribulations of this life. His grace will give you the power to run this race at a steady pace, leaving no trace of the ordeal you had to face. Visualize your achievements and create your destiny for a strong finish based on your faith. Always begin with the end in mind. Your ending will always be better than your beginning. Dreams won't work unless you do. Someone once said, "Inch by inch it's a cinch, but mile by mile, it's a trial." Take it one step at a time.

We Are All a Work in Progress

"I know what I'm doing. I have it all planned out - plans to take care of you, not to abandon you, plans to give you the future you hope for." (MSG)

"For I know the plans and thoughts that I have for you, says the Lord, plans for peace and well-being and not for disaster, to give you a future and hope." (AMP)
Jeremiah 29:11

*Our family decided to write our testimony acknowledging the journey that has taken us from a place of devastation to destiny. I can say whatever has come our way, we were blessed not to stray, but instead, we kneeled and prayed, for God said everything would be okay. Our family has been restored in the midst of a storm of afflictions.

"The thief's purpose is to steal and kill and destroy. My purpose is to give them a rich and satisfying life."
(John 10:10, NLT)

The definition of adversity is a state of serious continued difficulty or misfortune. You could say who showed courage in the face of adversity. Adversity is our university during our lifetime. The storms of adversity we all face are normal in life. Various storms come when you are expecting smooth sailing. It should be noted we need not fear because our Lord and Savior Jesus Christ is near. He is with us in our boat when the storms of life come our way. We are not alone. He is Emmanuel, God with us in the midst of every storm. The good news is storms don't last; they come to pass.

*Here are seven things our family learned from the storms of afflictions and adversity we experienced together:

1. Give Thanks At All Times

> *"And give thanks for everything to God the Father*
> *in the name of our Lord Jesus Christ."*
> (Ephesians 5:20, NLT)

Giving thanks to God at all times regardless of what we are going through is our salvation. We must learn to bless the Lord even when storms come to disturb our peace. It becomes a necessity for believers to maintain an attitude of gratitude.

> *"Remember the joy of the Lord is our strength."*
> (Nehemiah 8:10, KJV)

> *"Rejoice in the Lord always and again I say rejoice."*
> (Philippians 4:4, KJV)

These biblical truths are the secret to living a victorious life in Christ. God is doing great work in you. For God is working in you, giving you the desire and the power to do what pleases Him.

> "And I am certain that God, who began the good work within you, will continue his work until it is finally finished on the day when Christ Jesus returns."
> (Philippians 2:13, NLT)

> "So give thanks for the necessities of life and never take anything for granted that you have received from your Father in Heaven."
> (Philippians 1:6, NLT)

2. Reevaluate Your Priorities and Habits

> "Seek the Kingdom of God above all else, and live righteously, and he will give you everything you need."
> (Matthew 6:33, NLT)

Prioritizing and setting your habits in order is essential to spiritual development. We are creatures of habit, and changing a habit will take doing the same thing over in succession for at least thirty days. Deciding to change is not the easiest thing in the world. Change is mental as well as physical. It is going in the opposite direction, a one-hundred-eighty-degree turn. Speaking, ABOUT FACE as the army drill sergeant would say. Making rules for yourself takes time and effort, but in the long run, it is absolutely rewarding.

3. Check On Others Who Are Dealing With Adversity

> *"This makes for harmony among the members so that all the members care for each other. If one part suffers, all the parts suffer with it, and if one part is honored, all the parts are glad."*
> (I Corinthians 12:25-26, NLT)

Showing love to those who are dealing with circumstances and situations of life is of God. Lending a helping hand to exhibit mercy and compassion is a Christian characteristic. The biblical principle that is in operation is what you make happen for others, God will make happen for you as well. *"Christ said, Love the Lord your God with all your heart, and with all your soul, and with all your mind. This is the first and great commandment. And the second is like unto it, You shall love your neighbor as yourself"* (Matthew 22:37-39, NKJV). *"If someone says, 'I love God,' but hates a fellow believer, that person is a liar; for if we don't love people we can see, how can we love God, whom we cannot see?"* (I John 4:20, NKJV). Whenever and wherever we can offer aid and assistance to our fellow man is exactly what God would have us do.

4. Pray About Everything

> *"Don't worry about anything;*

instead, pray about everything."
(Philippians 4:6, NLT)

Tell God what you need, and thank Him for all He has done. In the gospels, Jesus instructed His disciples to pray. He gave them what is called the Lord's prayer as found in Matthew 6:9-13 and Luke 11:2-4. It is a model prayer, a prayer outline or an agenda as to how to pray and what things one should pray for.

Christ also revealed in Matthew 7:7-8, the three types of prayer.

- Asking is a petitionary prayer where we ask God for the things we desire Him to do for us.
- Seeking is a prospective prayer where we are attempt-ting to determine the will of God in what we are seeking from God.
- Knocking is a persistent prayer where we continually go to God in prayer through intercession.

Prayer is spelled A.S.K.: Asking, Seeking, Knocking. The Lord wants us to use these types of prayer as needed. It doesn't matter what we are facing; prayer is available for the believer to use as a weapon to overcome the issues of this life. Nothing can compare to the mighty power of prayer.

5. Relaxation and Exercise

"Physical training is good, but training for godliness is much better, promising benefits in this life

> *and in the life to come."*
> (I Timothy 4:8, NLT)

> *"Then Jesus said, Come to me, all of you who are weary and carry heavy burdens, and I will give you rest. Take my yoke upon you. Let me teach you because I am humble and gentle at heart, and you will find rest for your souls. For my yoke is easy to bear, and the burden I give you is light."*
> (Matthew 11:28-30, NLT)

Take a deep breath, and calm down. Inhaling and exhaling is always a good habit whenever things get out of control. Times of adversity provide you with opportunities to steal away and get quiet. Relax your mind, lay down, and take a nap. You'll be surprised just how much better you will feel. Resting is an instance or period of relaxing or ceasing to engage in a strenuous or stressful activity. We all need to take time out and stop working to recover our strength.

> *"Be still in the presence of the Lord and wait patiently for him to act. Don't worry about evil people who prosper or fret about their wicked schemes."*
> (Psalm 37:7, NLT)

When storms of adversity come your way, take the time to exercise and allow for some recreation.
For sure exercise has some health benefits that are listed here:
- Helps you control your weight.

- Reduces your risk of heart disease.
- Helps your body manage blood sugar and insulin levels.
- Improves your mental health and mood.
- Helps keep your thinking, learning, and judgment skills sharp as you age.

> *"Then Jesus said, 'Let's go off by ourselves to a quiet place and rest awhile.' So they left by boat for a quiet place, where they could be alone."*
> (Mark 6:31-32, NLT)

6. Communicate with Family and Friends

> *"Some friends destroy each other, but a real friend sticks closer than a brother."*
> (Proverbs 18:24, NLT)

> *"But Jesus said, 'No, go home to your family, and tell them everything the Lord has done for you and how merciful he has been'."*
> (Mark 5:19, NLT)

It is a blessing to have family in support of whatever you do. This has been our family model for years. As Dr. E. V. Hill used to say, *"A family that prays together, stays together and a child brought up in Sunday School is seldom brought up in court."*

No matter what, make sure you include your family and friends whenever possible. There are so many who would love to have the support of their family and friends. Jealousy and hatred can invade our relationships among family and friends, leaving severed relations.

*I thank God our family was able to show a united front. Starting as a young adult and raising a family was a difficult thing to do. It was always expected that the first family of the church had it all together. Being in public view didn't help because everyone could see all the faults and failures of our family. Pleasing the people with a public display became our custom.

It was difficult to get a family ready for church service every week. Our children were subject to the scrutiny of the families who made up the local congregation. Our close family ties presented the strong foundation that gave us the courage and pulled us through. Keeping a growing family together while dealing with attitudes and personalities within the household was like a juggling act. Things were tight but at the same time had to be kept right. The family routine caused us to act out our respective roles as if we were in a television series. The constant display of showmanship took its toll over the course of time. In the long run, we all realized the only certainty about our family was the fact we had each other. Thank God, my parents demonstrated a pillar of strength. We relied heavily upon them to keep our family in order. They weren't perfect.

At times, like any other family, we didn't have it all together. Because of their devotion to our family relationship, they brought us together as a team for continual development. Both of my parents were from large families. My aunts and uncles on both sides of the family were supportive in many ways. We had many cousins, but that didn't keep us from getting along with one another. Communication was an integral part of our family progression. At holiday events, the family would gather to thank God and enjoy meals for a wonderful family tradition. That time of fellowship made a lasting impression on all of us as we were encouraged to maintain these gatherings in the future.

Family reunions were held yearly, which included relatives from across the USA. A spirit of unity was celebrated among the family, showing respect to the elders of our heritage. Love could be felt among us as our family history was often rehearsed for the younger generation to capture the way things were done. Family fellowships set the tone for communicating the purpose and plan for our legacy. Sharing the achievements and accomplishments of various family members gave hope and inspiration to all. The commitment was made by the older family members to keep a spirit of pride about who we are and where we had come from. We were never allowed to accept mediocrity or exhibit a nonchalant attitude about anyone or anything. Respect was the main objective to one's self and giving those deserving honor. Spending time with friends allowed for positive conversation, which resulted in mutual personal developments.

7. Journal What You Receive

"Then the Lord said to me, 'Write my answer plainly on tablets so that a runner can carry the correct message to others'."
(Habakkuk 2:2-3, NLT)

This vision is for a future time. It describes the end, and it will be fulfilled. If it seems slow in coming, wait patiently, for it will surely take place. It will not be delayed.

Journaling our activities, achievements, and accomplishments during our lives is highly recommended. A journal is a daily record of news and events of a personal nature. It is also referred to as a diary. We are encouraged by the prophet Habakkuk to write down the things that occur in our lives. This is a wholesome habit. It provides us with a continual reminder of the great and marvelous things the Lord has done for us. Inspiration is needed today more than ever before, and it is provided by journaling.

People all over the world are hungry for encouragement to enable them to make it day by day. Sticky notes are used to remind us of little things that need to be done daily. God desires to impress upon us the need to daily consider His goodness and mercy. During times of adversity, journaling what you are going through with the testimony of victory brings glory to God. Writing down those wonderful things that have happened during your lifetime is a witness to God's amazing grace. *"The prophet Jeremiah declared, Thus says the Lord, the God of Israel: Write in a book all the words that I have spoken to you"* (Jeremiah 30:2, ESV). There is a purpose for writing or journaling what has happened. It is to record for the coming generation that the Lord is to be praised for His provision for His people.

> *"Let this be recorded for a generation to come, so that*
> *a people yet to be created may praise the Lord."*
> (Psalm 102:18, ESV)

In the Torah, there were commandments given requiring that words written by God were to be kept where all could read and live accordingly.

> *"And these words that I command you today shall be on your heart. You shall teach them diligently to your children, and shall talk of them when you sit in your house, and when you walk by the way, and when you lie down, and when you rise. You shall bind them as a sign on your hand and they shall be as frontlets between your eyes. You shall write them on the doorposts of your house and your gates."*
> (Deuteronomy 6:6-9, ESV)

I recommend scripture journaling. This is where you keep both notes on your study of the Bible and a record of things that happen in your everyday life. Over time, as you analyze and study the Word of God, you can apply what you've learned to your life experiences, which may make it easier to overcome difficult situations. It should be noted that by scheduling at the same time, journaling will become a natural and regular part of your agenda you can look forward to.

Here are several ways you can use your journal:
- Record daily events for later reference.
- Celebrate wins.
- Break down future goals and next steps into taking action to-do lists.

- Arm yourself with words of wisdom.
- Capture those brilliant ideas as soon as they occur to you.
- Take notes on things you read, hear, and watch.

Finally, here are some tips to help you get started with journaling:
- Try to write every day.
- Keep a pen and paper handy at all times.
- Write whatever feels right. Your journal doesn't have to follow any certain structure.
- Use your journal as you see fit.
- During the storms of adversity, we can activate these seven things to provide for us a way of escape leading to ultimate victory in Christ.

God is working on us. He began a work in us, and He's the one who will complete it. It is for our good that His construction uniquely molds and makes us into His image.

> *"It is certain that God has a plan for our lives. A plan is a detailed proposal for doing or achieving something. It also can be defined as an intention or decision about what one is going to do. You see, God has his plan and we have our plans. It should be noted that our plans and His plan usually don't match."*
> (Jeremiah 29:11, NLT)

Isaiah the prophet stated, "'My thoughts are nothing

> *like your thoughts,' says the Lord. And my ways are far beyond anything you could imagine. For just as the heavens are higher than the earth, so my ways are higher than your ways and my thoughts higher than your thoughts."*
> (Isaiah 55:8-9, NLT)

*I remember singing a song written by Joel Hemphill, "He's still working on me." It teaches the truth of Philippians 1:6 (ESV): *"And I am sure of this, that he who began a good work in you will bring it to completion on the day of Jesus Christ."*

The first verse goes like this,

> *He's still working on me*
> *To make me what I need to be*
> *It took him just a week to make the moon and stars*
> *The sun and the earth and Jupiter and Mars*
> *How loving and patient He must be*
> *'Cause He's still working on me.*

God's Masterpiece

This image of God working in us is woven throughout Scripture. In I Peter 2:5, we are Living Stones that the Lord is shaping, growing, and building up into a Spiritual House. We're left with a picture of the Lord, with a chisel in hand, cutting away the pieces that don't belong, fashioning us according to His plan.

> *"For we are God's masterpiece. He has created us*

anew in Christ Jesus, so we can do the good
things he planned for us long ago."
(Ephesians 2:10, NLT)

Here, we are described as God's workmanship, His handiwork, His masterpiece, as though the Lord is a painter and we are the canvas, where He creates a work of art for His glory. Whether you have been striving toward a Gospel family for years or just recently embraced the biblical vision of bringing the Gospel home, Scripture assures us God is not finished with us yet. He's the skilled craftsman, the creative artist, chiseling, cutting, shaping, painting, and sanctifying us and our families until His work is complete.

How do you know God is working in your life?

- God is working in your life when the fruit of the Spirit is visible in your Christian life.
- When you allow Him to use your talent or gifts to serve people.
- When you manage to have peace in the midst of the storms of adversity in your life.
- When He protects you and your family from hurt, harm, and danger.

So, from the inside to the outside, we are a work in progress. It takes time and temperance for God's work on us to be performed. God has patience as He works on us. He may smooth off the rough edges time and time again. The Lord will even start over and over until it is right in His sight. The Lord gave another message to Jeremiah. *"He said, 'Go down to the potter's shop, and I will speak* to you there.' So I did as he told me and found the potter working at his wheel. But the jar he was making did not turn out as he had hoped, so he crushed it into a lump of clay again and started over" (Jeremiah 18:1-4, NLT).

While God is working on us, He will allow afflictions to come. It is during these times we are in a stage of growth. Our lives are a work in progress where God allows external pressures. Progress means to develop to a higher, better, or more advanced stage. It is also a movement to an improved or more developed state. The old preacher said, "God will pull you through if you can stand the squeeze."

> "So the Egyptians made the Israelites their slaves. They appointed brutal slave drivers over them, hoping to wear them down with crushing labor. They forced them to build the cities of Pitham and Rameses as supply centers for the king. But the more the Egyptians oppressed (afflicted) them, the more the Israelites multiplied and spread, and the more alarmed the Egyptians became."
> (Exodus 1:11-12, NLT)

The enemy doesn't want what God is doing in your life to come to pass. Satan fights over time to keep our growth and development at a standstill. Surviving becomes our focus when the winds of affliction blow our way.

The Israelites were a major threat to the Egyptians. They outnumbered them and were growing at an alarming rate. So, they were enslaved and forced to do hard labor. Their task was to build cities from scratch.

That was done to crush their spirit, make them give up, and quit. But the surprising thing was that the more the Israelites were afflicted and oppressed, the more they multiplied and spread. That was alarming to their enemies. God continued to allow growth and development in the face of their enemies. They grew in number, and they also grew in their strength to endure. God blessed them in the midst of the storm of affliction. Now, that's what can happen when it seems we are overwhelmed by the circumstances of life. Their growth through multiplication promoted progress. Adversity reveals the gap between who you are and who you need to be. This occurs through patience, acting the same way all the time.

We should not let what we are going through hinder our growth, development, and continued progress. Sometimes, in our apparent weakness, we develop strength through the things we are dealing with, which makes us stronger. So, growth will put you in a position where you are uncomfortable. It will cost you something to grow. This is where character is developed.

> *"And I want you to know, my dear brothers and sisters, that everything that has happened to me here has helped to spread the Good News."*
> (Philippians 1:12, NLT)

The Growth Process

There's no doubt about it that sometimes things happen to us for the furtherance of the gospel. In other words, we grow through what we go through to the glory of God. A testimony comes from our stand in the midst of adverse conditions. Paul realized his suffering for Christ's sake brought about a greater witness for the kingdom of God. Therefore, consider the following factors that pertain to our growth in the Lord:

- All growth involves risk
- All risk involves change
- All change involves a loss
- All loss involves pain

We can grow in faith and confidence when things are seemingly out of control. We learn to trust God more fully when we don't know about the future. God holds the future. Whatever you go through will help you to grow, too. Our lives are not the total of one snapshot or photograph. Our lives are made up of many snapshots. Those snapshots when put together in successive movements develop into a motion picture that shows all from start to finish. I am reminded of the song called "Ordinary People," as sung by Danniebelle Hall.

Just Ordinary People
God uses ordinary people.
He chooses people,
Just like me and you
Who are willing
To do as he commands
God uses people that will give him all
No matter how small your all may seem to you

Because little becomes much as you place
it in the Master's hands
Just like that little lad
Who gave Jesus all he had
How the multitude was fed with a fish and loaves of bread
What you have may not seem much
But when you yield it to the touch of the Master's loving hand
Then you will understand how your life
could never be the same.

Our Father God meets us where we are and uses what we have left to finish the work He has started. Don't think about what you have or haven't done. Instead, think about what great things the Lord does for us.

"Come back to the place of safety, all you prisoners who still have hope! I promise this very day that I will repay two blessings for each one of your troubles."
(Zechariah 9:12, NLT)

Being a work in progress is a wonderful thing. It means you always have the chance to improve yourself and become better than who you already are. The King James Version of Jeremiah 29:11 ends with this phrase, *"to give you an expected end."* God begins with the end in mind. Before He gets started, He has already finished His work. If we are going to end strong, we must have a strong spirit, soul, and body. There must be joy in our journey. We are better than where we came from. Stop looking in the rearview mirrors of your past life. Look forward to the future. See the road before you. Keep your eyes on what's ahead through the front windshield. Thank God for the treasure that's in the midst of your trials. God can turn our mess into a miracle.

*My kids grew up loving pizza. I can remember going to the pizza house and ordering large pizzas. It was always amazing to me to watch the process of how a pizza is made. They begin with the dough. It is balled up, flattened and smashed out, thrown up in the air, and beaten by the handlers. Then, after all that, the various items are placed on top, and there it goes into the oven. Wow, all of that to make a quality pizza. Think about it, there was a rigorous process before my children could enjoy a delicious pizza, hot from the oven.

Life's experiences of difficulties, darkness, and doubt are all designed to rebuild and bring us to our final results. Ultimately, God desires to bring us to a new dimension in Him. It is during the physical process, which leads to our spiritual progress; the blessing of our perseverance pays rich dividends. Therefore, remember to do these things for an expected end:

- Call (pray) to God
- Listen to God
- Seek God
- Find the Lord when you have searched with all your heart
- God will turn your captivity and bless you with more than you had before.

"In those days when you pray, I will listen. If you look for me wholeheartedly, you will find me. I will be found

by you, says the Lord. 'I will end your captivity and restore
your fortunes. I will gather you out of the nations where
I sent you and will bring you home again to your land.'"
(Jeremiah 29:12-14, NLT)

"So that if anyone is in Christ, he is a new creature:
the old state of things has passed away;
a new state of things has come into existence."
(II Corinthians 5:17, WNT)

"'Yes, indeed,' Yeshua answered him, 'I tell you
that unless a person is born again from above,
he cannot see the Kingdom of God.'"
(John 3:3, CJB)

"Since you have been born again, not of perishable
seed but of imperishable through the living
and abiding word of God."
(I Peter 1:23, ESV)

Reflect

Rē•Bound: A Collection of Family Reflections

The Martin Family

www.ingramcontent.com/pod-product-compliance
Lightning Source LLC
Chambersburg PA
CBHW042116100526
44587CB00025B/4077